Acknowledgement

I would like to express my greatest gratitude to God Almighty for keeping me alive throughout all the challenges I had been through and for his blessings in my life. I appreciate and acknowledge the people who have helped & supported me during the storm of my life. I am grateful to my mother - Joyce Wanjiku for her continuous support at all times, ongoing advice & encouragement to this day.

A special thanks of mine goes to Dr. Connor O'Shea who helped in more ways than one to be what I am today. I appreciate and acknowledge the mentorship of Brendan Moore of National University Ireland and Rev Paddy Keary, Parish Priest for his great support and advice.
It has been a great honour and privilege to be trained by Rev. Eugene Curran, Head of School of Adult & Community Learning, All Hallows College.

I wish to thank everyone else that has helped and support me one way or the other in my life especially in many projects I have been involved with, you all inspired me and encouraged me to go my own way, without whom I would be unable to achieve this much.

At last but not the least I want to thank my friends who appreciated me for my work and motivated me and to God once again who made all the things possible.

GW00806305

Pastor Amos Ngugi
Acts of Compassion Ministry

Introduction

I have known Pastor Amos for the past 6 years and he has been a student of mine both at the Pathways exploring faith and ministry course at Emmaus Centre Swords and more recently as a student on Adult Learning B.A All Hallows College. Amos has drawn on his past experience and considerably on his experience in the pastoral field most notably with Acts of Compassion Ministry.

His approach in this book shows the Bible as the source both of practical guidance to avoid conflict and of theological insight. The biblical combination of ethics and theology can help to shape our thoughts, feelings, and actions.

In times of conflict our natural human emotions often try to dictate our behaviour. We feel anger and want to lash out. We feel fear and want to defend or attack. We feel wronged and want to get revenge. Yet if we allow our emotions to guide our behaviour, inevitably we will simply make matters worse. Conversely, if we tenaciously hang onto biblical teaching, we will find the power to act rightly even when our feelings try to drag us in the wrong direction.

Conflict will always arise, but we will do well to know how to avoid it by following the Biblical guidance contained in this book.

Rev. Eugene Carran
Head of School of Adult & Community Learning
All Hallows College (Dublin City University, DCU)

Table of Contents

How to behave
in times of difficulty

What should you do and where should you go during difficult times, During those hard times, it is so easy to forget where you are heading as your mind is so confused. With an increasing amount of random destructive events and financial turmoil occurring around the globe, there is always the question about what should be done. It is very easy to lose track of the good things that you have, loss of faith and hope are inevitable for some people.

Those questions that you ask yourself, should not be considered as weaknesses but seen as a sign of maturity to take the appropriate steps forward to find the solution to the problem you are facing. You should remember that what's happening is not unusual and you are not the only victim.

If your mind is troubled, it is advisable not to take any decision as often it will lead in the wrong direction. The best thing to do is to calm down, rest and pray, seeking God for guidance.
It is also an opportunity to renew ourselves, change our bad habits and improve ourselves.
Another negative behaviour is anger. When the solution to a particular

problem seems far away, you easily get angry and spread gossip.

This kind of attitude and behaviour demonstrates signs of .fear and discouragement. You may be very worried and cannot resist talking maliciously and negatively. It is important to remember that this does not make the situation better, instead it hurts others and spreads discouragement to others facing challenging times also.

The wounds grow deeper and a lack of trust takes place in the heart and mind. The problem seems to grow bigger and therefore it takes longer to solve. You are wounded and if left unattended it can lead to anger or resentment.

- *How can we handle matters during challenging and difficult times?*
- *Stay calm and keep focused.*
- *Do not panic.*
- *Search the mind and heart to discover where things went wrong.*
- *Difficulties can occur by your one mistakes or by outside circumstances.*
- *Pray and seek God's Guidance.*
- *Calmly but surely put all you energy and effort into working through the problems, which will in turn lead to resolution.*

Overcoming bad thoughts

*"Finally, brothers, whatever is true, whatever
is noble, whatever is right, whatever is pure,
whatever is lovely, whatever is admirable -
if anything is excellent or praiseworthy -
think about such things." Philippians 4:*

Your mind is like a battlefield with a constant open opportunity for all sorts of thoughts to enter. You think from morning till night unless you are sleeping.

What kind of thoughts are developed in your mind? It is said that a man's life is what he thinks about all day long. If your thoughts are evil, your behaviour and actions will also be evil and if your thoughts are good and pure, then good deeds will come out.

A plan, creativity, an idea, intentions and motives...every action you perform, takes shape in your mind first. then you act-upon them. You should not allow bad thoughts to take over in your mind even though you might be surrounded, by temptations which play tricks. When this happens, never give in. Instead take sometime to evaluate those thoughts. Always think about the aftermath "What will happen if I surrender?"

If they are not productive, if they do not bring anything good to your life, then it's time to change bad thoughts and behaviours. Overcome them and always pray for help which comes from above.

Why do we act badly?

It is so easy to choose an easy way to deal with problems. We rely on our thoughts and act upon them. Lying, instead of telling the truth, indulging in useless arguments based on what we see and hear without trying to find the source of the problem. Concealing important secrets instead of revealing them or even worse we blame others instead of taking full responsibility. This kind of attitude and response clearly shows the way we think. It is without a doubt a sign of immaturity and lack of responsibility.

- *Evaluate the thoughts coming into your mind.*
- *If they are bad, rebuke them.*
- *Always think of the consequences and outcome.*

Dealing with our bad actions, overcoming remorse

Our lives are many times littered with had actions we have committed in the past. We have hurt people on our way. We have acted badly towards those who lived peacefully with us. We may have betrayed a partner, a husband or wife by having an affair with someone who probably was an HIV victim. We may have been infected ourselves and now we infect our legitimate, true and sincere partner, husband/wife who shares our life.

How do we live and dope with them on a daily basis? Many people live with remorse and it affects them badly, it's a wound which they cannot heal.

The first thing is to acknowledge that we .cannot change the past. What has happened is in the past. What shall we do then? We should acknowledge that we are weak and cannot heal the wounds which destroy us like a cancer. It would not be a bad idea (if there is a way) also to ask for forgiveness to the person we hurt. If we cannot come face-to-face, then a few words in a letter or email could do the job. This is not always possible though as the person might not be alive or maybe he/she is now living in a different country.

The best thing is to leave it all in God's hand and ask for forgiveness.

It is our responsibility to deal with the issues in our life. We can either choose to live with remorse and remain bitter until death or we can choose to deal with it and live happily again. Always remember that free will to choose was given to us since the beginning.

- *Acknowledge our weaknesses.*
- *Remember that we cannot change the past.*
- *Forgive and ask for forgiveness.*
- *We have free will to choose.*

Find our weaknesses and know our priorities

When life is hard and hopes are lost, when we try our best and keep our faith bur still don't see am result, what do we do? How do we behave then? Are we depressed and turn bitter. Do we feel defeated and lose control?

There is one common mistake that a lot of people make , distinguishing between needs and wants. For instance we might say that "We need food and want a camera". We do not need a camera, food is the most important. Very often when people fall into despair, it is because they have not been able to identity their need or they simply mistook their want for need. They keep focusing on something they want and when they cannot obtain it, they despair, turn bitter and blame others. They choose to keep themselves busy instead of trying to figure out what went wrong and why they did not obtain the thing they sought after.

It is very important to pay attention to our priorities in life. Put first things first. By doing so, we will advance in life and avoid unnecessary stress and despair.

- *Identify our needs,*
- *Leave the things we want for later.*
- *Pay attention to priorities.*

We learn by our own mistakes

Who has ever lived a blameless life in this world? One passage of scripture puts it this way: "We all sin and fall short of the glory of God" Romans 3:23.

Everyone makes mistakes in life at some point. Sometimes it can be very painful followed by a deep feeling of guilt because we mess up our own life and others as well.

Many people tend to focus on their mistakes and feel sorry. This is not the way to go. Do not procrastinate. The best thing to do is to acknowledge that we indeed made a .mistake and messed up.

We cannot erase the wrong we did, but one thing we can do is to learn from it. As the saying goes: "We always learn through our own mistakes". We should turn that mistake from a stumbling block into a stepping stone and move on. Call it experience. Next time you will be sure you won't repeat it again.

As a result we should also consider changing our bad habits of doing things. If we are lazy, we should consider disciplining our lives and working harder. If laziness has brought defeat in our lives then we should work on that particular area to avoid another disaster.

- *Acknowledge our mistakes - do not bury them.*
- *Learn through our own mistakes.*
- *Recognise our bad habits and discipline ourselves.*

Substance use disorder

Many people experiment with substance use for many different reasons. Although substance use does not automatically lead to abuse, there are times unfortunately where consumers become totally dependent on it. No matter then how little or how often it is consumed, if it causes problems in life - at work, school, home, or in relationships - the person probably has a drug abuse or addiction problem.

Substance use can alter the way the brain functions. The changes which take place in the brain interfere with the ability to think clearly, exercise good judgement and control behaviour. Lack of concentration and loss of interest in valuable activities are also noticeable. Mood swings occur on a regular basis and the person feels depressed, useless, worthless and plunges into even more depression.

Victims. choose to be miserable and full of self pity rather than looking for help. Some go to the extreme by partaking in alcohol or drugs resulting in hallucination.

Drug abusers rend to conceal their symptoms and play down their problem. If a family member or friend is thought to be taking drugs then you should try your best to help him/her to get out of that trap.

- *Think ahead before engaging in substance use.*
- *Substance use affects the brain.*
- *Changes in personality and behaviour occur.*

Be a problem solver
in times of difficulty

In difficult times we procrastinate a lot, thinking about the size of the problem and wasting time and energy in worries and despair. We cannot control every difficult circumstance that comes our way or that occurs in our world, but we can control our thoughts and use our brain in a positive and appropriate way to cope with those difficulties.

Are you in the storm of life and have reached a place where yon can't take it any more. The problem is way beyond your limit to Solve it and you now start sinking in despair. That's the moment to throw yourself into God's mighty hands and let him take you through the storm.

Life is often unjust and unfair, favouring one group who do not deserve it and disapproving of others who deserve recognition. This should not be an excuse to turn your heart bitter. You should not let yourself be carried away by such unfairness and do wrong as this is a sign of weakness. First of all you should bear in mind that you are not the only one facing hard times in life. In one way or the other many people around the world face some kind of difficult times. You need to be positive, focused and believe that there is always a way no matter the odds surrounding us and how hard it may appear. In those particular moments faith should be the mechanism which produces the energy and the desire to face and conquer the difficult situation. Throw yourself in the hands of God.

Prayer and action should follow. It may not be immediately but if we continue to press on patiently, we will surely obtain a solution.
- *Do not despair - keep believing.*
- *Keep focused and press on.*
- *Be patient - God is in control in your life.*
- Be positive.

Self confidence and preparation are the keys to fulfil dreams and have a brighter future

Everybody has dreams and wants them to be fulfilled; hut dreams are nor fulfilled by pure magic or luck, Preparation is the key for it to become true. This is easier to say than to do but it is a fact that whatever you want to achieve in life will need, days or years of preparation. Many-people do not achieve their goal because they give up in the middle of the road due to hardship and outer circumstances. Only those who press on will succeed.

The secret to success is hidden in the daily preparation. It is no doubt the only sure way. There is no short cut in life. Another important thing to do is to set your mind to success. If you believe that you can succeed then you have to work your way through to your success. You need to close your ears and eyes to negative things. Outer circumstances may tell you that it is difficult; you might see that there are obstacles around you but if you have set your mind to succeed then nothing will be impossible. Do not meditate on those negative thoughts which tell you "it is difficult" but concentrate on what you are doing. Avoid being negative and speaking negative words. Words are powerful and can negatively impact your life. Always confess positively that "everything is possible" when you try hard.

- *Keep believing that success is yours.*
- *Close your ears and eyes to negative thoughts.*
- *Set your mind to success.*
- *Work hard and do not give up in the middle of the road.*

Learn how to deal with anxiety

Anxiety does not know any borders; it affects people of all ages in all countries,When situations are difficult to control and you cannot handle them anymore you start being anxious. Our mind is a battlefield where victor}1 is won or lost, so it is good to think before acting in any difficult situation. You have two choices regardless of how hard the problem appears to be: erne is to give in and live with it and the other is to learn to overcome it.

By giving in you discover that you will continue to suffer and feel unhappy whereas learning to overcome your anxiety will give you more energy to look for the solution.

Besides, anxiety wastes your time and energy both mentally and physically, You cannot solve any problem when you are anxious.
Learn to control your thoughts. If you lack control over your thoughts, anxiety grows stronger.

Develop self discipline and learn to control your feelings as well, because feelings and emotions fuel and strengthen anxiety.

In the morning for example, first thing you need to think about are the good things that are happening to you. There are always some good things happening, even if small and insignificant.

Start the day by confessing positive words or simply confess the word of God. Tell yourself how you would like your day to be. Use positive, cheering and motivating words.

Keep yourself busy when anxiety takes control of you. Activity keeps your mind off your anxiety. When you wake up in the morning, start doing something right away, and keep busy all day. Whatever that activity is, be it cleaning the house, washing the dishes or working in your garden, reading, studying, meditating, or exercising your body, it will keep you away from anxiety. Staying idle and thinking about your problems and worries won't make them go away.

Set a goal and work everyday to achieve it. This action will direct your thoughts and feelings away from worries and anxieties, toward something more positive and constructive.

Be courageous
to confront issues

What is courage?

Courage is the mental and emotional confidence and ability to deal with difficult, challenging and sometimes seemingly impossible circumstances. It is the ability to confront tear, pain, danger, uncertainty, intimidation and other threats.

When faced with a difficult situation, it is wrong to procrastinate or choose not to do anything to solve the problem and direct our anger towards others and blaming them for our lack of courage.

Why we should develop courage?

Courage is like the spiritual and/or emotional power with which we persist to obtain a result. With it we confront problems and deal with adversity head on. It is indeed a psychological muscle that helps us deal with life's challenges.

How to develop courage?

Making effort to develop courage is like building strategic ways to successfully live your daily life in a constructive and positive way. It is a step towards taking responsibility of not allowing your mind to trouble you nor to allow challenges to defeat you.

"We must have courage to bet on our ideas, to take the calculated risk, and to act. Everyday living requires courage if life is to be effective and bring happiness".

Dealing with compulsive obsession

Compulsive obsession is an anxiety disorder characterised by intrusive thoughts that produce uneasiness, apprehension, fear or worry. Symptoms of disorder include excessive and repetitive activities like washing or cleaning, checking. Obsessive compulsion could be time consuming and can render a person even more distressed especially when they are aware of it. They might also he paranoid and potentially psychotic.

Sometimes stress - even though it does not cause compulsive obsession might trigger obsessive and compulsive behaviour, and stress can often make obsessive-compulsive behaviour worse.

If you think that you suffer from obsessive compulsive disorder then you might seek help. Your condition might be translated into uncontrollable thoughts, irrational urges of feeling compelled to perform the same rituals over and over again. There is a variety of help available. The first step would be to do some research and educate yourself on the matter.

Self Help Treatment
- *Physical exercise on a regular basis.*
- *Adopt a healthy eating habit.*
- *Avoid alcohol and nicotine.*
- *Get enough sleep.*
- *Stay connected with family and friends.*
- *Join an OCD support group.*

Making better choices

Almost everything we do in life is a choice. To get out of bed in the morning is a choice. To go to work, do your job, pay your rent, take chances and risks are all choices. To eat unhealthy foods knowing you will gain weight, increase fat and cholesterol and be at risk for heart disease are all choices. To get married, stay in an unhappy marriage or have children, again all these are our choices.

Every choice has a consequence
Sometimes the consequences are good, 'sometimes they're not. Either way, there is always a choice and a consequence that goes along with. It is empowering to realize and exercise your ability to choose. That's a whole lot better than leaving your life to chance.

As awful as the options may be, there is always a choice. If you choose to go out with friends or colleagues when you know you should be preparing for a test or a presentation, that is your choice. If you don't pass the test, or you don't do as well as you know you were capable of on the presentation, you will know you really have no one to blame but yourself. That's called taking responsibility for our actions.

Each time we make a choice, it moves us closer to or further away from something. Where are your choices leading your life? When you are facing a challenge or an opportunity ask yourself, "Is this going to bring me closer to or further away from what I want?"

For whatever things you want in life you always have to make a choice. If you want more money you have to make choices that will provide you with more money. If you want a better relationship, you have to make choices that encourage a better relationship.

Keeping yourself happy
in the midst of trouble

Keeping yourself happy and relaxed in the midst of trouble is a real gift as it is not an easy task. Very often happiness is associated with wealth, luxury and the bank account. There are people around us who appear to live the ideal life but are in fact very unhappy. On the flip side there are also people whose lives are hard, struggling day in day out hut are yet very happy.

What's their secret? It all depends on how they view situations. It is the state of the mind rather than outer circumstances. Some people know how to stay focused and keep" doing what they do to achieve then goals no matter if outer circumstances say the contrary. For others unfortunately, they are so disturbed by those negative situations that they become fearful and are "paralysed". They are doubtful and see impossibilities. Hear brings worries and stress in a person's life, it robs happiness and goals remain unfulfilled.

When fear takes place in a person, it blocks the way to success. Why? Because Fear is troublesome. It disturbs the state of mind. Each step which should be taken is mixed with uncertainty. "WHAT IF I DON'T...?" Enthusiasm is lost and the vision of life disappears. Fear prevents you from having fresh ideas. Bear in mind that challenges are unavoidable. When you fear and worry you cannot receive fresh ideas on how or what to do to overcome this challenge and move on.

To keep yourself moving on and happy, you will have to stop tearing and worrying. You have to learn to be relaxed and to focus on ways to overcome the challenge or to find an alternative to continue your way to success.

- *Keep your mind from trouble.*
- *Keep focused.*
- *Do not fear*
- *Relax.*

Never give up in life

L ife is an endless battle. Human beings are like soldiers on the battlefield, facing all kinds of challenges in all areas of life. Will you give up because of that? Always ask yourself the question? "What if everything was given to me on a golden plate with no challenge at all? No effort to do, no sacrifice at all?" What if you were receiving everything with such easiness on a golden plate? Would you be happy? Let me tell you that life would be so easy that it would turn boring and make your world dull.

Challenges are here to test you, to make you grow bigger, to train you to bigger challenges and teach you some philosophy along the way.

See yourself as a body builder heading towards a gold medal. Body builders are challenged by weights. The heavier the weights, the more difficult it becomes, the greater the victory. Ask any body building champions about their training and they will tell you how hard it is but yet they do not give up. They do not just set up goals but they patiently work out every single day, have a proper balanced diet and plenty of sleep. Those who do not give up receive their reward.

Life is the same. You have a God given gift but because you give up easily when the least problem hits you do not achieve your goal. It is true that sometimes there are things that cannot be achieved by yourself nor can it be reached by education but it can be fulfilled by the power of God.

The goal once achieved, should not be kept for yourself, but what has been learned along the way can be shared with others. To be generous and care for others is important for God to fulfil His plan in other people's lives.

Do not be afraid

Never be afraid and he dismayed in this world. No matter what happens in the world. It is very frustrating when things go wrong and when we hopelessly battle against hardship with no solution. But we should be courageous and trust God and still move on. Anxiety troubles the mind and prevents you from seeing afar.

Anxiety plunges people into despair. They are so anxious that their mind Cannot work our properly how to find a solution. They lack patience and become vulnerable to traps the devil sets in front of them. For instance a person who has applied for several jobs without any answer might fall into drugs dealings and robbery because he/she is so desperate.

They are so anxious about bills to pay and shopping to be done that they jump into anything thrown at them. A lack of integrity corrupts the soul. Watch out and be careful. Life has the appearance of being too hard to handle but be patient. If it's too hard then seek God in prayer and He will lead you to the right place where you will be peaceful and relaxed to work out in your mind and you can be rest assured that you will not fall into the trap of the adversary.

Sometimes God tests our integrity as well. Learn to stand on firm ground and do not sin. The problem is not just the lack of integrity but that sometimes by yielding to the trap of devil we can't see how badly we lack it.

- *Do not be afraid.*
- *Do not yield to the devil's trap.*
- *Remain firm.*
- *Anxiety makes you vulnerable to-.the enemy.*

What Is your attitude towards your own mistakes?

What do you do when you make mistakes? Do you fed guilty endlessly and feel sorry for yourself? Do you procrastinate and feel frustrated any time somebody reminds you of your mistake? Well, we all make mistakes and each time we think of them we are uncomfortable and wish we could go hack in time to erase them.

What is done cannot be undone. You just need to put it aside and move on. It is easy to say, but it's not easy to forget. True statement" but first of all bear in mind that nobody is perfect and as long as you live you will make mistakes willingly or not, because of our human nature. Secondly making a mistake, big or small, is not the end of the world. There is still room for forgiveness and improvement.

Refuse to quit, don't give the devil permission to sabotage your destiny and your dream in life.

What is your attitude towards mistakes? Are you learning from them? Obstacles can't destroy your vision but attitude can.

Learning from our own mistakes
You can learn from things when you are willing to ask. You can choose which direction you go based on what you can see.

Quitting is not an option. Discouragement or negative thinking can blind you from achieving your goals in life.

When you try to avoid failures you do not learn from your mistakes.

Solving the problem of comparing yourself with somebody else

It is always good to take time to analyse the nature of a problem. How it happened? Why it happened and how serious it is before tackling it. You have to figure out whether you need help or if you can handle it without any support.

Do not try to compare yourself with others. Everyone is different and behaves differently to the same or different circumstances. It might discourage you to see someone being able to tackle the same problem that you struggle with. Do not try either to be someone else. Each person has a different path.

Start by saying that you are who you are and what you want to become.

Everyone on this planet wants to achieve his/her goals and craves for appreciation. It is the deepest principle in human nature.
By trying to compare yourself to someone else you cannot achieve your goals.

When you receive help from someone who contributes to your success, always be thankful.

Do not run away from
the storms of life

R unning away from the storms of life will make you a failure instead of a winner. From time to time God allows storms in your life in order to shape and mould you. Unfortunately many people do not understand that.

God is a sovereign God and He can use the storms of life to change your heart or lead your path in the correct direction and save you from a pitfall.

Through a storm He might lead you to people who will he your friends and help you to fulfil His plan. God works in wonderful ways. He might want you to acknowledge that you should not neglect your real friends who could have a positive contribution to your life. Maybe you never realised the importance of friendship.

Many times we do not know the value of things or the people around us unless we lose them and then we are full of regret.

- *Learn to appreciate friends.*
- *Do not run away from the storms of life.*
- *Let God lead you.*
- *The storms of life can bring a new direction.*

Things which
make you frustrated

How many times have you thought of giving up because the situation is too hard? Do not give up but Be steadfast no matter how hard and impossible it may appear. If you choose to become bitter because of the difficulties you end, up hurting yourself and those around you.

This will without a doubt shut the door to happiness.

If you choose to be resentful or if you hold a grudge or experience a sadness like bereavement because you lost someone unfairly or unjustly, you will turn bitter and develop frustration. This will have such a deep impact on your behaviour that you will start losing self respect and your best friends, noticing your new and strange behaviour, might choose to stay away from you. Frustration will pile up over time and by the time you discover it you will be a totally different person filled with negativity. All this might prevent you from achieving your goals in life.

Hurting yourself and others is considered as a social sin and it surely does not benefit the doer nor the people around him/her.

- *Do not give up.*
- *Self respect.*
- *The choice to act positively is yours.*
- *Be steadfast.*

How to deal with shame

First of all shame is getting the feeling that something is wrong with you and it's usually tied to your self worth. To be able to deal with shame, it requires that you understand where the shame comes from, why you feel shameful and the difference between shame and guilt.

Guilt is an emotion that you experience when you violate your own values hut shame is a feeling that tells you that you are not worthy or not adequate.

If guilt stems from realising that you have made a mistake, shame comes from believing that you are a mistake.

Sometimes people can make you feel ashamed by being critical about you. That's because they were raised by overly critical parents who made them feel ashamed about themselves. Those same people in turn criticise you when you make mistakes and try to make you ashamed of your wrong deeds without having cruel intentions because they are programmed to think that way.

Getting rid of shame
Listen to your inner self, acknowledge any feelings of inferiority and inadequacies that you find.

The next time you meet or face a situation that makes you feel ashamed, remind yourself that you are only feeling shameful because of your old wound and that your past has no control over your present.
Respond to those who try to make you feel ashamed: If someone attempts to make you feel ashamed about yourself reply quickly and assertively. It you reply with confidence and assertiveness then instead of doubting yourself the person who criticises you will start to question the validity of his/her critical comments.

The value of things in your life

The value you place on something means the price you would pay for it no matter what, whether it is a car, house, education, pleasure ETC.

Don't involve yourself in petty issues which take a lot of your time. Use your time wisely because the time that you lose cannot be recovered in days, months or years.

Losing time in idle or useless things can result in anger and bitterness leading to violence and abuse which can affect other people around us. You might indulge in unnecessary arguments thinking that you are right and always putting others down. This kind of behaviour will make you lose friends and you cannot build a proper relationship with anyone.

- *What are the things you value most?*
- *Use your time wisely.*
- *Time lost cannot be recovered.*

The battle of the mind

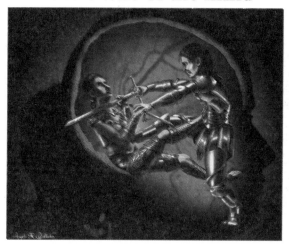

O ur mind is a battlefield and what we see and hear affects the mind either positively or negatively. You should learn to accept the positive things and reject the negative ones as the negative ones might become a hindrance to your success. To transform shame into respect you need to work hard and pay the price to achieve your goals and don't agree with everything that life throws at you. For example shame, inferiority etc.

Fear and shame are very powerful and they can take control in your mind if you don't right them. Life is sometimes cruel, if you are assaulted with negative criticism from other people quite often, don't allow your mind to accept them otherwise you will be depressed.

Different kinds of fear

- *Being alone.*
- *Feeling rejected.*
- *Fear of death.*
- *Fear of embarrassment. Don't allow it to play a major role in your life - trust God.*
- *Be positive.*
- *Reject negative words from others.*
- *Work hand for your success.*

Every man
has a purpose in life

The most miserable person on earth is not someone who lacks money or education or is homeless but one who does not know his/her purpose in life. We are all here to fulfil a purpose and the greatest one is the relationship you have with God. When someone does not know his/her purpose in life then the latter has no meaning at all.

A person without purpose is lost and sometimes shameful. If you choose to carry this shame on your shoulder it Will hold you back and prevent you from achieving your success,. There is always a way. You must constantly search for it until you Find it and get on the right track again.

Always pray and ask God for wisdom as wisdom will lead you to fulfil your purpose in life and fulfil God's plan. Wisdom is like a bag that you have to carry with you always and some people realise this and it guides them through managing their time.

- *Know your purpose in life.*
- *Ask for wisdom to fulfil that purpose.*
- *Never give up.*

Don't let yourself be manipulated when taking important decisions in your life

Do not let any one manipulate you when making important decisions in your life. It seems very easy for people to advise you on such and such matters. They appear to be expert in giving counsel but one thing you should ask yourself, even if it appears to be good, is it applicable to your situation? Each and everyone has a different way of looking at a particular situation and they tend, to give counsel based on the way they see things. That does not mean that what they tell you should necessarily be applicable to you and your situation even though they seem good.

Some tend to put pressure on you as well as if they are right and that you should do accordingly. If you agree with what people tell you and you give in to those pressures you will act foolishly and miss your own goals and will regret it later.

When you give, in to pressure and you compare your actual situation to those in the past filled with mistakes you have made, you become doubtful and questions start to play tricks on your mind:
"What if my friend is right?" "I made that mistake in the past now 1 should not do this and that" "Maybe I should listen to him/her".

When this happens you become vulnerable and allow yourself to be manipulated. It messes with your important decisions and it can destroy your future as well.

- *Be firm when taking decisions.*
- *Do not allow yourself to he manipulated by others.*
- *Listen to advice but do not give in to pressure.*
- *Be yourself*

Do not give up

Giving up is not an option in life, Responsibility is the key. You need to know who you are -and where you are (heading to).

Do not judge too quickly the situation in front of you and make up your mind that it is difficult and that you cannot continue. Always remember that perseverance is the road to success.

Winners are those who have taken the decision to continue their way to success, no matter the odds around them and even if life shows some negative stuff. They are focused and their mind is set to success.

- *Always think carefully before acting.*

In everything be thankful
and do not complain

Life is not always easy; you are sometimes misused by unscrupulous people. Are you upset because of that? Are you complaining because someone has disappointed you?

There are people who from morning till night complain about everything and are never happy with what they have. If you are healthy, then give thanks to God because many people are not able to enjoy a healthy life. Be happy and make the most with what you have while at the same time working on improving yourself.

If you have a problem with always complaining, then you have to fix-that by looking at what God has done in your life and what you have where others don't.

Is complaining good sometimes or is it always bad in your own views? Consider your moods after complaining and examine if it benefits you. If not then there is no reason to complain as nothing good comes from it.

- *Stop complaining.*
- *Give thanks for what you have.*
- *Make the most of what you have.*
- *Slowly work your way through to your improvement.*

Do not be too harsh on yourself

We need to learn to accept ourselves. You are who you are, made in the image of God. Don't be harsh and judge yourself. If you are aware of a particular area or areas that you have to work on to improve yourself, then do so and stop beating yourselves; because of those weaknesses.

Learn to let go of your past, make the most of your present and press on to improve your life and achieve your goals.

- *Do not judge yourself.*
- *You were created in the image of God,*
- *Forget your past and press on to achieve your goals.*

Look for ways to improve yourself rather than gossiping

Do not he seated with gossipers. Gossiping is simply idle talk or rumour about the personal or private affairs of others. Gossiping is very harmful and docs not help to improve yourself or solve any problem. It is better to be lonely than to be seated among gossipers.

Instead of gossiping there are marry other constructive things which can be done. For Instance you can self discipline yourself on your diet, exercise regularly and learn a new skill instead of wasting" time.

When you hear of a new idea, embrace it and immediately start to apply it in practice while discussing. Do not procrastinate but get straight to the point.

- *Do not be seated among gossipers.*
- *Gossips do not solve problems.*
- *Look for constructive things to do.*

What image do we have
of ourselves?

Sometimes you hear different information about yourself. People observe and make an analysis of your personality and it is difficult for you to accept their conclusion concerning you because it tears you apart. To some degree you agree with the way people see you but not always.

What is your attitude to their comment? Do they affect you? People who are easily discouraged by failures cannot achieve their goals in life. Bear in mind that you can learn new coping strategies to deal with your failures.

Dealing with grief

Many people who have experienced grief feel that time was a healing factor for them. Indeed, time has lead to recovery in many cases.

The primary treatment for a grieving person is talking and you can help that particular person by listening to his/her experience and how she feels.

Problems are normal and are among the major means God uses to conform us to His image so that we can grow to trust Him only.

Life: the best teacher ever

Can you share the joy of others easier than how you can share their pain? Or does their pain remind you of your own? Theirs are so deep that you cannot stand their presence and you need to get away as that pain triggers your own.

You must bury the past. Acknowledge what happened and accept that you cannot change the past but only forget it. If you don't, then you stay with it and its old hurts, Just learn front it and move on.

Life is the best teacher ever. Through its many challenges and hurts that you sometimes create or which come to you unexpectedly, life teaches good lessons that are worth taking on board to learn and grow.

Press on for your success

Don't walk backward into your future. Happiness can be more than that of your past life so let the past life go away from your mind. Many people tend to stop in the middle and get discouraged as they are pressurized by the odds around. If you do so you will never achieve your goal.

Aggressive behaviours: "Why do many people like to be in; the circle of safety and secure base?

Vision

Vision: The human eye is an extraordinary complex organ. Truly it is a gift of God. If someone is asked and given an opportunity to add additional organs to their body many will choose to have an eye.

How do we behave when faced with challenges?

Shouting, violence, abusive behaviour, putting others down: Your behaviour is a function of your decisions not your condition. You are responsible for your own life. You choose to handle hard situations either in a very comprehensive way with calm and confidence or you can choose to be impatient and aggressive towards others.

Why do people cry? People cry when they are happy or sad. It is a natural emotional response to certain feelings, usually sadness and hurt, but people cry under other circumstances as well, The pressure you face everyday from new challenges in your life make you cry sometimes and you need to work hard to get new answers everyday.

The difference between who you think you are, how you view yourself and how people see you in your communities are three different things. Your attitude, behaviour, friendliness/coldness, the way you handle difficult matters or tackle a situation says a lot about you.

- *What's your response to challenges?*
- *How do you tackle hard situation?*
- *Your behaviour and attitude say a lot about you.*

What are your plans
for the future?

What are your plans? What do you intend to do in life? Have you set your mind up to achieve your goals? How are you preparing the way leading to your achievement? You may he tempted to trade in your old dreams when they seem difficult and unreachable but they may be dreams many people find hard to achieve in easy ways. So if you have been given a talent and dreams and you know what to do to reach the summit, don't give up.

Cast your burden to God. Have you ever lost your dream and find yourself in a challenging environment and isolation? If so then trust God, pray and He will give you ideas to fulfil your dreams.

Treat others the same way you want them to treat you

INTIMACY

Observe each individual that you encounter, and analyse what needs they may have and then try to meet those needs. The human being is a very complex creature. Feelings, emotions* sense are part of the-human beings. The way you treat others and make him/her happy. Others will hate you or love you depending on the way you treat them. Even when they hurt you, you still-have the choice to understand why they did and treat then) gently. By doing so, you are releasing a positive energy and might bring them to change their bad behaviour and repent. If you are always resentful and devalue or point out faults to others without trying to understand why they behave or act in such and such a way, if you treat them like common objects people will give up on you.

Unreliability, immaturity & doubt

Unreliability, immaturity and doubt are Characteristics of people who are ignorant and Who did not grow up even when they learned things the hard way. They are people who could not see a better future and are comfortable in that situation. Instead of seeing challenges and difficulties as stepping stones to grow and move on they have chosen bitterness and anger. Those types of people never go far in life as they are always doubtful of themselves. If you are in that situation today, you might end up opening doors to misfortune and invite all sorts of evil things in your life.

Remember that you are responsible for your life and the way you think. The way you think and Judge things lead you to take actions accordingly. If your thoughts are pure and positive your actions will be fruitful and benefit yourself and others whereas negative thoughts and judgements will lead to negative actions and you will destroy others on your way.
Be careful of the things you say to others. If you are a messenger of bad news in bad times you will hurt the broken hearts and completely destroy the tiny faith of those already facing hard times.

- *Immaturity leads to nowhere.*
- *Turn your challenges into stepping stones.*
- *Do not he a messenger of had news in bad times.*

What's your vision or purpose in life

The most miserable person on this planet is not the one who is poor, uneducated or homeless but the one without, vision or purpose. You are on this, planet for a reason, like everyone else you have a duty to Fulfil. It is a talent or creativity that you need to develop which will be useful for yourself and others.

So what is your vision in life? Ask yourself right now-what are you doing with your life? If you feel a kind of calling and know deep from the bottom of your heart that you need to fulfil your duty then do not waste time. Work hard on it so that you will not lead yourself to regrets later.

Always work your way patiently through to success and do not quit. Quitting is not an option. Do not get discouraged as discouragement or negative thinking can blind you and prevent you from achieving your goals in life.

Once on the summit, do not turn selfish. Remember that others directly or indirectly contributed to your success. It is your responsibility to take care of others now and lead them to success. Good deeds to others is always rewarding.

- *Fulfil your duty.*
- *Do not quit when things go wrong.*
- *Once successful do not remain selfish but help others in their to success.*

Keep pressing forward even in times of trouble

Don't he discouraged when facing giant problems. You might see that a problem is too big to solve and that no matter what you try, it's to no avail. Bear in mind that you still need to keep your faith and keep hoping, that there will be a solution. By doing so you are setting your mind up to receiving fresh ideas -which flow from within. It is the spirit of God guiding you but if you are agitated you cannot receive ideas. Even when everyone is running away from you, if you keep your faith and keep pressing forward, your victory will be great and those who run away from you will see it from a far.

Never cease to trust God. It is a fact that there are situations which are too big and difficult to deal with. In that case you need help. You cannot rely only on your limited ability to solve difficult problems. You can't get there by yourself. You must rely on God especially in all our persecution and tribulation that we endure.

When your life is in a pit and loneliness and failure walk side by side with you, and struggling is part of your daily life, it is easy to doubt the existence of God. That's where you should encourage yourself and grow stronger than the problem you face. How do you do that? By thinking positively and confessing God's word of encouragement.

- *Do not be discouraged.*
- *Keep your faith.*
- *Keep pressing forward.*
- *Do not rely on your own ability.*

Forgetting the past and pressing forward

"A man without vision shall perish" Proverbs 6:2. You might travel from country to country, have the best job and the best house in the world but if you have no vision and don't know your purpose you will be carried away by the wind and things of this world. If you feel too guilty arid keep carrying your past mistakes, this will always be a hindrance to your success. The past is pone and you don't need to reap anything from-it thinking that you deserve a better life.

Do not run away from difficult situations. They keep coming your way time and again. Instead listen to advice with an open heart and mind, gather all information appropriate to your situation and apply them for a better solution. Always plan in advance, be ready like a soldier on the battlefield, when moments of trouble come your way you will be equipped to fight back. Set targets and work hard to achieve your goals.

Do not be negative and behave badly when things go wrong or when someone hurts you. It is never rewarding. Instead of finding solution and mending broken relationship among friends you end up destroying it and friendship is destroyed forever. Always remember that friendship is a gift from God, when it is broken we have to mend it and not destroy it completely. Be a problem solver not a solution destroyer.

- *Know your purpose*
- *Keep pressing forward*
- *Be a solder on the battlefield*
- *Face challenge and a problem solver*

Always be specific in the things you want to do and apply wisdom

There are many waste-timers in this world who roam about not knowing their purpose. Be in the field of education, family life or career. They move one step forward to two steps backward and sideways and yet there is no change. In the morning they want to go west, they choose to be in the south in the afternoon and end up in the north at night and still don't know what they want for their lives.

If you are in that situation you need to pray and ask for wisdom, The bible clearly says that: "if any of you lacks wisdom, let him ask of God, who gives to all generously and without reproach, and it will be given to him." James 1:5

Wisdom will reach you discipline and guide you through the proper steps to take towards your goal. Wisdom will deliver fresh ideas on how to prioritise your work and also the ability to fulfil each task with courage and determination. When your mind is well organised and all your plans are in order you are on the way to success; you cannot fail.

Good planning and hard work leads to prosperity. Do what is right and just.

- *Do not waste time roaming about.*
- *Wisdom will teach yon discipline.*
- *Have a well organised mind.*

A journey based on wisdom

LIFE JOURNEYS

Seeking Destiny

Conversations With High Achieving Women In Kenya

Compiled by Susan Wakhungu-Githuku
Photography by Bobby Pall

William Shakespeare: "Where as in a theatre, the eyes of men, after well-graced actor leaves the...'

In this life we are all actors and we are fulfilling a duty. Once done, we are gone.

Preparation is the key to anything we want to achieve in life. We start our journey by asking God to give us wisdom. Why do we need wisdom? Wisdom is the master of instruction. Wisdom will teach us how to plan and organise our lives based on our priorities. When challenges come our way, wisdom will show us what action to take and when. It will help us to handle hard situations, tackle a particular problem, deal properly with a cold hearted person and so on...

Wisdom will give us ideas about the steps to undertake to achieve our goals. Wisdom will also help us to look beyond the barrier of problems and see the solution from afar.

Wisdom will turn us into an advisor and a problem solver. It will lead people to us because we will have the wisdom and knowledge to provide solutions.

Wisdom provides us with good planning in our journey and when we complete our journey we end up in prosperity.

How to tackle situations in the proper way

The Best way to handle things when they are fall trig a part is to stay cool and maintain you sense of humour then agitated in times of trouble, a person loses his/her means to think ahead because of panic and worries. The mind Is troubled and instead of finding the appropriate solution, things get worse and hope is lost. Whereas calmness gives inspiration and hope which increase faith. A calm mind is able to think ahead and organise ideas to tackle problems.

Problems come in different ways. It could be financial, difficult family relationship, broken relationship, bad news or a failed exam... whatever way, the victim/s are always put under stress. The problem appears so big that the victim loses hope and quits fighting. Many choose to indulge in binge drinking to forget the problem but this does not bring a solution, instead it has greater consequences. It does not matter how deep the hurt and loss appear, you still need to keep fighting, forget the past and move on. If the pressure is too big, look for something constructive to do like going out to meet friends, do some jogging or simply talk to someone whom you know you can trust and give you advice. Change your thinking.

- *Do not quit in times of trouble.*
- *Stay calm for inspiration.*
- *Keep the good faith and keep fighting for your achievements.*

How do you cope with things that are bothering you?

When you lack direction in life, you are worried and fear lies at your doorstep. You dread failures and struggle tiny in day out, trying your best to succeed. Be relaxed and work your way through to success. It you arc well organised and prepared then you should not he afraid of failures.

How do you react to bullying? Do you know that bullying is the type of destructive behaviour aimed at a person But the aims of Bulling is to undermine and abuse.

Do you react and try to fight back. Do you insult him/her and fall into the trap the bully set up for you? Because that is what he wants. He wants you to get angry so that he has a reason now to bully you even more. Bullies feel inadequate and threatened by you. You probably have a creativity or talent that the bully does not have and he wants to have it. Bullies cannot come face-to-face to ask you for that creativity or talent that you have and it annoys him/her. The only way bullies cast their frustration is by treating you badly.

One thing you should do it you are bullied is to ignore the bully. Let him fool himself. Bullies do not realise that when they bully others they are in fact telling you that they are frustrated and inadequate.

Before taking any decision in life, always evaluate the pros and cons. If things go wrong, bear in mind that you are the only one who pays dearly for it. Think twice and seek advice, as it is a wise thing to do so that you won't regret it afterwards.

- *Do not fear but be relaxed and work your way to success.*
- *Bullies are to be ignored*
- *Think twice before taking any decision in life.*

The benefit of friendship

What is friendship? Is it important in our society? True friendship is perhaps the only relationship that survives the trials and tribulations of time and remains unconditional. A unique blend of affection, loyalty, love, respect, trust and loads of fun is perhaps what-best describes rhe true meaning of friendship.

The three dimensions of love.

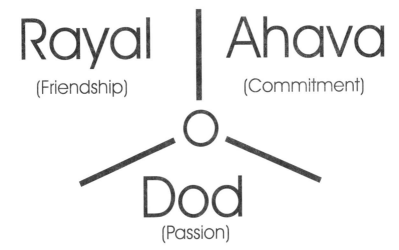

Rayal
(Friendship)

Ahava
(Commitment)

Dod
(Passion)

Our identities are shaped by a force beyond our control. The degree of our control on our present circumstances is limited. Society though contributes a lot in shaping and moulding our lives. Society for instance tends to define what jobs will be done by which family members. Within the family, each has a different role to play helping and supporting one another.

Society expects us to get married formally. A given culture or society helps to define what values families deem important.

Be patient till the end and do not blame others if you don't make it

You have been waiting for an answer to a problem but gave up waiting or pressing forward just at the moment you were about to receive your reward. Why? It is -due to a lack of impatience and discouragement. Do not give up but wait until the end. If you do so, you might be turning your back on your dream and miss the opportunity which will eventually lead you to the fulfilment of your dream. Do you know that our words have either a negative or a positive impact.

Do not get bitter and give out to others. Positive as well as negative words wound people and also break down a person's spirit. DO not blame your failures and impatience on others.

Always be sincere and honest towards people as it keeps your spirit free and your heart happy. Also you won't fear because you are genuine in all your ways. People who are hypocritical destroy others with negative and unproductive words. Careless words spoken can damage relationships with friends and families. Therefore we need to be careful and think twice before uttering a word.

- *Be patient, do not give up easily.*
- *Be careful before uttering a word.*
- *Be always sincere and honest.*

Don't worry
about what people think of you

People are ashamed when they fail and always think about what others will say about them. They feel intimidated and sometimes avoid friends and families because of that. Know that failures are often part of success. Consider the saying "we learn by our own mistakes". It's alright if you have made a mistake and it led to your failure. Take it as a lesson, learn from it and grow. Don't be afraid of being rejected. You are not alone in this world. Everyone without exception fails in life. Always remember that.

If you have failed an exam or a family relationship, do not be discouraged. Organise your thoughts, plan ahead and stand up on your feet and start afresh. Refuse failure and do not fear that you will fail again. You are not going to make the same mistake again. Besides do not let outside circumstances intimidate and stop you from going ahead.

Live by your principles and always know and respect your boundaries. We are not super humans who can do all things. We have abilities as well as limits. For instance we cannot all be doctors, lawyers, pilots or artists. We have different talents. So know your talents and remain in your own shoes. Trying to live in somebody else's shoes will lead you to disaster and you will regret it.

In other words don't do things which are not your job and which you don't have any experience of, because there will be consequences afterwards.

- *Don't wrong about people's opinion.*
- *Do not be afraid of failure.*
- *Live by your principles and do not try to live in someone else's shoes.*

If you are faithful in small things you will be responsible for even greater things later in life

If you have been given a small task, he happy and do it with love. Be faithful in what you have to do and do not complain. Be it a job, an opportunity to study or simply a simple task to help others, always be thankful. Remember that you are being given an opportunity to be useful and helpful. Faithfulness always brings rewards.

People around you watch your attitude. They watch the way you do things; how you handle difficult situations and your response to each task. The way you behave and respond towards such situations and people says a lot about yourself. Actions speak louder than words.

- *Fulfil your task with love.*
- *Be faithful in the least possible task given to you.*
- *Your faithfulness in small things will lead you to great responsibilities.*

Living an aimless life is a waste of time

If you live an aimless life, you will never achieve anything in life. You will be miserable and be frustrated especially when you see others climbing the ladder of success. If you have a dream or hope that you can improve your life, then don't kill what you can keep alive and be an attentive listener, Be attentive to opportunities raising around you, seize and use it for your own benefit.

Now that you know your purpose and are working hard on it, do not let people oppose you by listening to their opinion regarding that particular matter. Sometimes people might revive your past mistakes just to discourage you; close your ears to those negative words and open your ears only to good things.

You might be listening to advice or appear to be listening but if you close your mind and reject good advice, you will be the loser. Always rub shoulders with people who will give you good advice and help you to build your life. Never rely just on yourself.

- *Living aimlessly will bring you nowhere.*
- *Seize every opportunity coming your way.*
- *Close your ears to negative words and open them to positive ones.*
- *Always listen to good advice.*

Listening

Good communication surely begins with good listening skills. Strong listeners are more empathic and are better at solving problems: If you want to be a good listener, then consider the following: wait for the person to talk, after that ask empowering questions, be patient, and remove all distractions, keep focus.

Barriers of listening: some common barriers and ways to minimize them.

Noise - Many times it is difficult to have a meaningful conversation due to a noisy location. Noise comes in many forms: from people, equipment, street noise and more. If it's too difficult to hear and focus is lost, move to a quieter place.

Visual- it can be tough to concentrate when there is a lot of activity or other visual distractions In the area. As with noise, move to a place where there are less visual distractions when required.

Stress - it is Hard for someone who is stressed to pay attention to what is said. The mind of a stressed person is worried and thus makes listening difficult. He/she might appear to listen but the message- does not get through. Stress can happen for many reasons such as family issues, .work problems, financial concerns, illness of self or a family member, and more. Refocusing frequently works. If it doesn't (and the conversation is important), then choose another time to talk.

Time - a pressing appointment (for either you or the other person) won't allow adequate time to address an issue effectively. In such cases choose a more convenient time.

Reflective listening is a communication strategy involving two key steps: seeking to understand a speaker's idea, then offering the idea back to the speaker, to confirm the idea has been understood correctly.

When you listen reflectively, you express your desire to understand how the person feels and thinks. You believe in the person's ability to understand the situation, identify the solution and worth.

You respect other people's feeling and show your desire to offer your support. You are not judgemental but share how others perceive what they say or do.

Stay firm and do not
be carried away

Don't let yourself be carried away in emptiness when you end up achieving nothing. When life is hard and appears to offer you nothing but trouble; you should still press forward. Your true faith will be known in moments of temptations and trouble.

It is easy to have faith when things go perfectly well in life. What happens when everything goes wrong and-hope is nowhere to be found? You have faith when you walk on velvet, but where is your faith when troubles come your way?

Always be prepared like a soldier on the battlefield so you can stand firm when an avalanche of challenges comes your way. You need to be equipped and plan ahead so that when challenges come your way you pass through them with courage and determination. You will then overcome all obstacles that prevent you from achieving your goals.

Good things and bad things happen for a reason. When good things happen to you, enjoy and give thanks. When bad things happen, do not mourn but patiently analyse the situation, what went wrong, why it happened, what you can learn from it. It's a way to grow. The bad thing can actually teach you something - who knows? See the positive-side of it. You should learn to look beyond the troubles and hope for the best result.

- *Stay firm in moments of trouble.*
- *Be prepared like a soldier on the battlefield.*
- *Be always ready to face challenges.*

Don't waste time in
Unproductive activities

Time is precious. The 10 minutes gone are not to be recovered. So don't involve yourself in petty issues and useless activities which take a lot of your energy and do not bring anything fruitful to you or others.

Know how to manage your time and look for productive activities to do, like learning something new, reading a book, learning a new skill etc. Gossiping, involving in unnecessary discussion, being bothered about others are things of no values.

You need to plan ahead and do something important with your time.

If you have a dream, talk to someone who will share your vision and help you. While choosing someone to share your dream with, you should also pay attention to his/her response to see if that's the right person to help you. You need to pay attention to their body language and attitude when you share your dreams. Also listen attentively to what is being said.

Your feeling and experience of pain, suffering, shame, guilt and a sense of failure might lead you to isolation and turn you into a time waster. Those things put great pressure on and become a hindrance to your success. If you are in that situation, do not sit down and lose yourself in thinking but stand up and do something. The past is behind, look ahead. You cannot repeat the same mistake and feel the pain again.
You can't be happy when you are passing through shame and guilt so it's better to leave them behind.

- *Time is precious, do not procrastinate.*
- *Use your time to be productive.*
- *Leave the past behind and press forward.*

Anger

A nger is a strong feeling of annoyance, displeasure, or hostility. It is an automatic response to ill treatment. It is the way a person indicates he or she will not tolerate certain types of behaviour. It is a feedback mechanism in which an unpleasant stimulus is met with an unpleasant response.

Some people are also very bad tempered and get angry just for anything which according to them is not correct. A person who gets angry all the time cannot think ahead because he/she is always under tension and lives in an atmosphere which is not peaceful and conducive to finding a solution.

Anger closes doors of opportunity because it prevents someone from having inspiration to solve a particular problem or to seize an unexpected opportunity. Anger blinds you so that you cannot see ahead and it harms both the angry person and others involved.

If you get angry easily, it will be known even if you try to hide it. You might appear, calm from the outside but because there is a storm inside of you, it always explodes sooner or later and people will then see your anger.

Anger can result in people losing their respect for you and it is a dangerous ground to tread on. Run away from anger.
- *Be always calm.*
- *Never lose your temper easily.*
- *Anger can close the door of opportunity.*